HUNTING AND FISHING

GOING DUCK HUNTING

BY FELIX PETERS

Gareth Stevens
PUBLISHING

Please visit our website, www.garethstevens.com. For a free color catalog of all our high-quality books, call toll free 1-800-542-2595 or fax 1-877-542-2596.

Cataloging-in-Publication Data
Names: Peters, Felix.
Title: Going duck hunting / Felix Peters.
Description: Buffalo, NY : Gareth Stevens Publishing, 2027. | Series: Hunting and fishing | Includes glossary and index.
Identifiers: ISBN 9781482482553 (pbk.) | ISBN 9781482482560 (library bound) | ISBN 9781482482577 (ebook)
Subjects: LCSH: Duck shooting--Juvenile literature.
Classification: LCC SK333.D8 P484 2027 | DDC 799.244--dc23

Published in 2027
Gareth Stevens Publishing
2544 Clinton Street
Buffalo, NY 14224

Portions of this work were originally authored by Tom Carpenter and published as *Duck Hunting*. All new material in this edition was authored by Felix Peters.

Designer: Joshua Olson
Editor: Noah Riccardi

Photo credits: Cover, p. 1 Sam Keckeisen/Shutterstock.com; p. 4 Brian N. Rogers/Shutterstock.com; p. 6 andipantz/iStockphoto; p. 8 Suzi Nelson/Shutterstock.com; p. 11 Konjushenko Vladimir/Shutterstock.com; p. 12 Steve Oehlenschlager/Shutterstock.com; p. 14 konstantinks/iStockphoto; p. 17 Vlad Kol/Shutterstock.com; p. 19 Steve Oehlenschlager/iStockphoto; p. 20 BulentGrp/iStockphoto; p. 23 nwbob/iStockphoto; p. 24 Iaroslav_brylov/Shutterstock.com; p. 27 muratart/Shutterstock.com; p. 29 York Museums Trust.

Printed in China

Some of the images in this book illustrate individuals who are models. The depictions do not imply actual situations or events.

CPSIA compliance information: Batch #QS27GS: For further information contact Gareth Stevens at 1-800-542-2595.

TABLE OF CONTENTS

CHAPTER 1
HISTORY OF THE DUCK HUNT 5

CHAPTER 2
FINDING DUCKS 9

CHAPTER 3
SETTING UP FOR A SHOT 15

CHAPTER 4
SAFE HUNTING 21

CHAPTER 5
CONSERVATION RULES 25

FACT FILE
PUNT GUNS 28

Test Your Knowledge · 30
Glossary · 31
For More Information · 32
Index · 32

CHAPTER 1

HISTORY OF THE DUCK HUNT

People have hunted ducks for thousands of years. For example, early American Indians created **decoys** out of reeds and twigs. When ducks came to the decoys, hunters shot the ducks with bows and arrows. They also caught ducks with nets or snares.

Hunting blinds help hunters hide from ducks.

In Europe, hunting for ducks and other birds is often called shooting.

When European settlers began moving west across North America, they used guns to hunt ducks. At first, they shot ducks only for their families to eat. But then hunters started shooting millions of ducks to sell in cities. Hunters targeted **migratory** ducks. Duck hunting became a booming business. However, it took a toll on duck populations. Numbers of ducks dropped dangerously low.

By the early 1900s, **conservation** efforts had started. Laws set up specific hunting seasons. People could hunt ducks at only certain times of year. It became illegal to hunt ducks that were migrating. As a result, duck populations began to grow.

Today, people hunt ducks in many places around the world. Some hunters eat the ducks they hunt. Others hunt as a hobby. Hunters often hide in a **blind** until ducks get close. Then they use a gun to try to shoot a duck.

CHAPTER 2

FINDING DUCKS

Hunters use decoys to attract ducks. Each decoy is attached to a string. A small weight keeps the decoy from floating away. A set of decoys is called a spread. To make spreads seem realistic, duck hunters blow on duck calls. Each call is designed to attract a certain kind of duck.

Wooden decoys are carved to look like different species of ducks.

Duck hunters often carry a variety of calls with them.

Many duck hunters use boats to set out their decoy spreads. Some hunters use flat-bottomed boats. These boats have motors that can navigate shallow water. Other hunters paddle in canoes or kayaks.

Hunters often wear waterproof clothes such as **waders** and hip boots. These items help hunters stay dry while they place decoys on the water. **Camouflage** clothing helps hunters blend in with the area around them. Hunters often use blinds to hide and wait for ducks, too.

There are two main kinds of ducks to hunt. Puddle ducks swim in shallow

Hunters often use boats to move around while hunting.

waters, such as marshes and ponds. Puddle ducks tip their tails up in the air to eat water plants. Mallards, teal, wood ducks, and pintails are puddle ducks.

Diving ducks live on lakes, rivers, and bays. They dive down into the water to get food. Diving ducks typically eat plants.

At approximately 14 inches (36 cm) long, buffleheads are one of the smallest kinds of ducks that people hunt.

They may also eat fish, clams, or shrimp. Ring-necked ducks, redheads, buffleheads, and canvasbacks are diving ducks.

Many hunters use pump-action shotguns or semiautomatic shotguns.

These guns allow hunters to make rapid follow-up shots if the first shot misses. A duck hunter's shotgun is loaded with shells. These shells contain pellets. The pellets are also called BBs or shot. They spread out in the air when the gun is fired. This gives hunters a better chance of hitting a fast-flying duck.

LEADING A DUCK

Ducks fly quickly. This makes them difficult to hit. Hunters wait for the ducks to come very close before firing. They also aim their guns ahead of the ducks before pulling the triggers. This is called leading the duck. Leading helps a hunter hit the duck instead of shooting behind it.

CHAPTER 3

SETTING UP FOR A SHOT

Scouting is the process of looking for a good hunting spot. When scouting, hunters use binoculars to watch the skies and water. They look for places where they think ducks are likely to be. Potholes are good hunting spots. These dips in the ground can often be found near large marshes. Many potholes are filled with water.

A swamp or pond can be a good place to find ducks.

Ducks often come to small potholes to escape other hunters.

An **oxbow lake** or a **slough** near a river can also be a good hunting spot. Points are good places to find ducks, too. A point is a piece of land that sticks out into a larger body of water. Ducks often have to fly past these places.

Puddle ducks will eat in grain fields. Duck hunters place special decoys in harvested grain fields. Then the hunters hide in small bags or structures known as layout blinds. When ducks fly in, the hunters jump out and shoot.

All ducks are challenging to hunt because they can see everything as

Hunters in layout blinds often wear camouflage clothing.

they fly over hunters' hideouts. However, ducks tend to land facing into the wind. Smart hunters put the wind at their backs. This allows the hunters to see the ducks coming. The ducks will come in close for a good shot.

When setting out a spread, hunters place the decoys so that incoming ducks have a place to land. An effective decoy spread will have two groups of duck decoys with an opening in the middle. The hunters wait at the opening.

Hunters must hide from the ducks while they wait. Some hunters crouch

DUCK DOGS

Many duck hunters bring hunting dogs with them. Labrador retrievers, golden retrievers, and Chesapeake Bay retrievers are popular breeds. These dogs swim out into the water and bring back the ducks that hunters have shot. Plus, dogs can help catch ducks that have been hit but are still trying to get away.

Hunting dogs bring ducks back to hunters.

in vegetation such as cattails, grass, or brush. Others build blinds out of wood. Then they cover the blinds with cattails, reeds, or branches. These blinds often have seats. Some even have heaters and places for hunting dogs to sit.

70 mm
70 mm
70 mm

CHAPTER 4

SAFE HUNTING

Hunting partners line up side by side to shoot ducks. It is important for hunters to plan where each member of their group will stand. Hunters should also plan where each person will be aiming. Each person should choose a shooting zone. A shooting zone is an area where only that person will shoot.

Hunters should handle guns and ammunition carefully.

Hunters should discuss their shooting zones before hunts begin.

Duck hunters should also wear life vests when wading in water. Many hunters also wear waders that have quick-release buckles. This allows a hunter to get out of their waders in just a few seconds.

SAFETY RULES

To avoid accidents, hunters of all ages should always follow four gun-safety rules. First, treat every gun as if it were loaded at all times. Second, always point the muzzle in a safe direction. Third, be sure of the target (and what is beyond it) every time the gun is fired. Fourth, keep fingers outside of the trigger guard until ready to shoot.

Following safety rules around guns helps hunters prevent injuries.

That way, the waders will not fill up with water and cause the hunter to drown.

People often go duck hunting in cold or rainy weather. Coats and hats help hunters stay warm. Waterproof gloves help keep their hands warm and dry.

CHAPTER 5

CONSERVATION RULES

Each year, governments help set the duck hunting season. The season tells when it is legal to hunt ducks. The season is at a different time each year. That is because it is designed to protect duck populations. Each year, the hunting season changes based on how many ducks are in an area.

US duck hunting seasons are between September and March. They can be no longer than 107 days.

Duck hunters can hunt only during certain dates. They must not hunt too many ducks. Each hunter must stay within the bag limit. A bag limit is the number of ducks that a hunter can shoot in one day.

In some places, each person must also purchase duck stamps before hunting. Duck stamps are US postage stamps that have artwork of ducks on them. In the United States, money from these purchases is used to help **preserve** duck **habitats**.

Hunters can also protect ducks' habitats by using nontoxic shot. When hunters fire shot, some of it falls into the water. Lead is poisonous to ducks and many other

The Federal Duck Stamp program has helped preserve more than 5 million acres (2 million ha) of wetlands.

animals. Animals that eat lead shot could get sick and die.

Nontoxic shot does not contain lead. It is made of steel or other metals. Using nontoxic shot helps ensure that ducks will fill the skies for many years to come.

FACT FILE

PUNT GUNS

During the 1800s, hunters shot so many ducks that the birds nearly died out in North America. These hunters used methods that are against the law today. One example was the punt gun.

Punt guns were giant shotguns. These guns were 10 feet (3 m) long and could weigh 100 pounds (45 kg). People attached them to small boats called punts and aimed them at flocks of ducks floating on water. Using this method, one hunter could shoot more than 50 birds with a single shot.

Punt guns helped hunters kill huge numbers of ducks at once. This overhunting put duck populations in danger. So, in 1918, the use of punt guns became illegal, and duck populations recovered.

A man stands with his punt gun in the early 1900s.

TEST YOUR KNOWLEDGE

Take this quiz to test your knowledge.

1. Write a paragraph describing how hunters can help protect duck habitats.

2. Would you rather hunt puddle ducks or diving ducks? Why?

3. Which type of shotgun shell is poisonous to ducks?

   A. steel
   B. iron
   C. lead

4. Why should hunters discuss shooting zones before the hunt begins?

   A. so that all hunters can have the same shooting zone
   B. so that two hunters do not accidentally choose the same zone
   C. so that each hunting dog can be assigned to its own zone

Answers can be found on page 32.

GLOSSARY

blind
A hideout in natural vegetation.

camouflage
A pattern that is designed to look like its surroundings.

conservation
The careful protection of plants, animals, and natural resources so they are not lost, ruined, or wasted.

decoys
Imitation ducks that hunters use to attract real ducks.

habitats
The places where plants or animals normally grow or live.

migratory
Animals that are moving from one place to another.

oxbow lake
A U-shaped lake near a river.

preserve
To protect something so that it does not change.

slough
A wet, muddy place.

waders
Waterproof boots and overalls that a hunter can wear to stay dry when standing in water.

FOR MORE INFORMATION

BOOKS

Bailey, Diane. *Small Game Hunting*. Minneapolis, MN: Lerner Publications, 2024.

Simons, Lisa M. Bolt. *Go Duck Hunting!* North Mankato, MN: Capstone Publishing, 2022.

WEBSITES

Britannica Kids: Duck
kids.britannica.com/kids/article/duck/390384
Learn more about ducks here.

National Geographic Kids: Mallard Duck
kids.nationalgeographic.com/animals/birds/facts/mallard-duck
Learn more about a common type of North American duck at this site.

Publisher's note to educators and parents: Our editors have carefully reviewed these websites to ensure that they are suitable for students. Many websites change frequently, however, and we cannot guarantee that a site's future contents will continue to meet our high standards of quality and educational value. Be advised that students should be closely supervised whenever they access the internet.

INDEX

bag limits, 26
blinds, 7, 10, 16, 19
buffleheads, 12

decoys, 5, 9–10, 16, 18
diving ducks, 11
duck calls, 9–10

habitats, 26
hunting dogs, 18–19
hunting seasons, 7, 25

leading, 13

mallards, 11

nontoxic shot, 26–27

points, 16
ponds, 11
potholes, 15–16
puddle ducks, 10–11, 16

scouting, 15
shells, 13
shooting zones, 21–22
shotguns, 12–13, 28

waders, 10, 22–23

Answer Key: 1. Answers will vary; 2. Answers will vary; 3. C; 4. B